T0381339

ANGELS
EVERYWHERE

G. Brown-Johnson, C.O.T.K.
(A CHILD OF THE KING)

Edited by Dr. Sylvia Cunningham

REVIEWERS:

Pastor Lonnie Johnson
Minister Jennifer Joyner
Blanche B. Layne

Angels are looking and keeping watch around the world to serve and make what seems to be impossible, astonishingly believable. Get excited because, wherever God is, the *Angels* are with Him. This confirms: *Angels* do exist! In addition to the *Angels* illustration in the book **"A City Called Heaven,"** it is acknowledged there is the presence of **"Angels Everywhere!"**

In God, the creator of us all, there are surprising and unpredictable possibilities with *Angels* which are remarkably real. Yes, these possibilities, beyond every imagination, take place by God's created *Angels*, A.K.A., His miracle servants. Miracles happen continuously because God made the *Angels* to help us.

It is appropriate to know about all of God's creation, especially His *Angels*. **We are not alone. Angels are now present with us.** Know that *Angels* may look in silence, with their eyes wide open and are attentive for considering every movement which will give us, (believers) the ability to reach and fulfill God's purpose.

Angels only act at the command and authority of God as *ministering servants.* They have no gender, and are available to help us with the ability to help others. Still, all of our help comes from the Lord. By doing what is necessary, at God's will, *Angels* work for completing His mission by those on earth. Not by natural means but in the *supernatural* presence with God. Not as a matter of course as the ordinary, but extraordinarily there are **"Angels Everywhere!"**

When following the directions written in a book called Holy, "*divine forces*" are transmitting visionary development supernaturally. Our Creator God is also called Holy. Written in God's Holy book, "The Bible," there are appearances of *Angelic* activity. According to (Revelation 5:11; 7:11) *Angels* are seated around God's throne. These seated around the throne are Angelic observers and are exceedingly numerous. *Angel* existence is accepted by those who believe that God is our very present help.

Biblically, Angelic activity tells of men, women and children who could only do what God requests successively with the presence of *Angels* **(Cherubim, Seraphim, Guardian Miracle Messengers, Ministering Spirits)** (Isaiah 37; Ezekiel 1; Hebrews 1:14) guiding along the way. *Angels* also called **Guardian Angels** and **Mighty Warrior Angels** are created to shield against the forces of evil which come upon us. *Angels* are here on earth for doing God's will with us. According to Psalms 91:11: The Lord has given His angels charge over every believer and God keeps us in His care (Matthew 18:10 and Acts 12:15). Believers really do have **Guardian Angels that may appear as a stranger, (Angels unaware – Hebrews 13:1).**

When God ask you to do an assignment, there are *Angels assigned to help.* Talk with God, for *"Angels"* are listening and are ready to work. A multitude of Angelic forces are here now and come near to us from around the throne of God to assist when there is a need in every situation. The power of *Angels* is divinely incredible, imagine that.

We make decisions, as humans, but ultimately God chooses those dedicated with commitment in doing His will to glorify Him. We too, like the **"Angels Everywhere"** are servants of the living God. Humans serve and act by God's Authority through reading, studying and doing what is written in His Word. Doing what is written is called "obedience," actions which are right, pleasing God.

Angelic forces are most observant in the earth realm and also live in heaven. It is good to know that right now *Angels* guide and protect from forces of evil or that which attempts to hurt us. From God's heavenly throne, *Angels* are sent out to help in every situation, spreading blessings from powers that are invisible.

Yes, *Angels* are God's miraculous *messenger servants* and aids mankind with safety and protection from danger. **Don't be afraid for God has not given us the Spirit of fear but His Spirit of love and power to do right in Him** (2 Timothy 1:7). God's *Angels* have *supernatural powers* whenever it appears to be any impossibility, the *Angels* serve on behalf of those who believe, all things are possible.

Spiritual by nature, *Angels* are filled with God's strength and wisdom. God made each of us and has assigned His *Angels* to watch us, that we will be able to fulfill His purpose. Specifically, there are **"Angels Everywhere!"** Standing next to you now is a good Angel. They may appear action filled wherever and whenever there is a need. Even when we are not able to see the *Angels*, they are present. Sometimes *Angels* are revealed, transforming themselves to look just like a man, a woman or a child. There are sightings of **"Angels Everywhere,"** serving us only from ruling orders given by the Creator God to fulfill His mission.

Open your eyes and visualize God's created *Angels* who are ready to serve those who believe His purpose is to be completed. *"Angels Everywhere"* are looking and watching even now and sent by God that we may receive what is needed when things seem to be difficult. Be reminded, *Angels* may appear as we are, and will walk along side us. They are there to pick us up, when we have fallen. When tears come or something happens that makes us cry, *Angels* are available to comfort us. We may not be able to see, but there are *"Angels Everywhere!"*

For example: remember that time, when running there was a fall causing a cut on your finger or knee, it seemed when Mommie kissed it, "wow," it felt so much better, and the tears disappeared ("thanks Mom!"). Just like the *Angels*, created to help us become better. When we are helped through difficulties by Dad; Mom; Grand dad; Grand mom; Sister; Brother; Aunt; Uncle; Cousin; Friend; Neighbor, Teacher or others may also have a spirit like the *Angels*. In times of emergency, either may "help," (or perhaps by someone not known). The response is: an *"Angel"* came and provided what was necessary. If someone known, forget not their thoughtfulness, give a card of appreciation and or to say two kind words: *"Thank You!"*). NOTE: *Angels have the Spirit of giving in time of need!*

God created *Angels* who are like He is — — Good. "Doing good and helping others is the activity of God's *"Angels Everywhere!"* *Angels* are present with God to do good. Laugh if you must, but it is the Truth. When help is needed, call on God and *Angels* come with Him to help! Thank God for being our very present help, along with His *"Angels Everywhere!"*

It is also very important to never forget, *Angels* are not to be – "worshipped!" They too are created and only worship the Lord, along with us. As *Angelic* messengers they make sure every task is accomplished for God's Glory. *Angels* have the ability to think and are able to talk. Listen closely they are also singers. As ministering spirits, *Angels* have their own identity, serving God's people and most times are invisible, but may appear in human form when necessary. *Angels* aid us as God commands them to do so. Call on God, *read the Text, His Holy text message!*

God hears our call according to His word, and answers in His time.

Share with others about the *Angels* who live in God's great presence and receives God's commands with us. Others will understand, by His Word, that we are becoming transforming servants, in order to please Him. Doing as He asks us to do, by faith, now called believers, we are being shaped daily in the image of God, and do not walk by sight, but know the truth that God is our Creator and we worship Him.

Believers worship only the true and living God (Colossians 2:18). Remember, *Angels* are not to be sought after for worship, neither are we to pray to the angels or any other. In the divine realm of faith, *Angels* pray with us, and, in our favor, miracles happen. *Angels* are celestial (extraordinary) beings, now listening and do the commands of our Creator God, who is our Father. When we pray say:

Our Father,

which art in heaven,
Hallowed be thy Name.
Thy Kingdom come.
Thy will be done in earth,
as it is in heaven.
Give us this day our daily bread.
And forgive us our trespasses,
as we forgive those that trespass against us.
And lead us not into temptation,
but deliver us from evil.
For thine is the kingdom,
the power, and the glory,
Forever and ever. Amen.

God created **"Angels Everywhere,"** for His purpose and only He delivers us from evil. There is no other greater than our God, who is *"Awesome."*

In the end of time, as we know it, we shall all see God, along with His heavenly *Angels*, and will also be judged by our Creator. From day to day always remember that not only here in this earthly realm, it is written, that there are in the heavenly realm, *Angels* bowing around the throne in God's presence saying *"Holy, Holy, Holy"*. *(Revelations 5:2; 11; 12:7; 14:6, 17)*. We are God's Holy people and presently alongside us are **"Angels Everywhere,"** assisting the increase and power of God's kingdom in us. These *Heavenly messengers* created and are now positioned for service from around the throne of God. The nature of angels is spiritual and angels are filled with God's strength and wisdom. Every good and perfect gift, comes from above. As we ask and seek direction each day, *Angels* of the Lord are available with us to serve with determination. Oh, what **good news** it is to know that we live in the presence of *Angels*.

There are also Archangels (Michael and Gabriel). The Archangels have a "higher" position with Supreme Authorities as ordered by God. Use supernatural imagination for seeing the presence of **"Angels Everywhere"** as they minister with supernatural power according to the will of the Lord.

Believe by faith, all things are indeed possible. **With God nothing is impossible!** Read it yourself, **it is not a vain imagination!** There are historical sightings of the **"Angels Everywhere,"** as revealed series of signs, manifestations with appearances in visions and dreams. Let us further explore the reviews from the Holy book, the Bible, by a few experiencing these supernatural servants, directly from the throne of God as extraordinary beings, seen and unseen. Yes, they still exist, here and now as -- **"Angels Everywhere!"**

Abraham & Sarah

Abraham & Sarah visited by *Angels* in their old age were told they would have a child. His wife Sarah, laughed so hard when she heard what was said, because she was an older woman who had passed the time for having a baby (Read Genesis 18:12-14). When the child is born, Abraham would become the father of many nations.

Every believer in God is the seed of father Abraham. A promise fulfilled by God, Abraham is the father of faith for all believers. The Creator God has *Angelic* forces surrounding us that we will also know what will happen in the future.

JACOB – A Warrior

Jacob, a servant of the Lord, was on a journey and took a moment to rest. While resting, laying his head on a stone, Jacob fell asleep and dreamed of — *"Angels"* on a ladder, going upward towards heaven (Read Genesis 28:10-22).

In the dream while the "*Angels*" were going upward, there were also "*Angels*" walking, on that same ladder, coming downward to the earth. When Jacob woke up, he said, **"the Lord is in this place". There are "Angels Everywhere."**

MOSES – The Deliverer

Moses by His **Guardian Angel** was protected from evil. The King of Egypt ordered that all boy babies, one year old and younger be destroyed. Moses was chosen to fulfill God's mission and was saved.

When he was born his Mother Jochebed placed him in a basket on the Nile River in Egypt to save him from death. Moses sister Miriam watched the basket as it floated along the river to make sure Moses was okay. Moses was rescued from the Nile river, by Pharaoh's daughter, taking him as her son. Moses was educated in the court of authority and became a strong leader in Egypt (God's *Divine* plan - Exodus 2:5)

God's chosen people needed *deliverance*. The *Angels* provided assistance to help God's people. God heard the cry of His people and he wanted them to be free to worship Him. Moses, called the "Deliverer," was inspired to become a leader with an angelic message from God, "the I am that I am," to tell Pharaoh -- *"I Am said, let My people Go that they may worship me."* (Read Exodus 9:1, 13).

As a believer in God, we too have a message to share with others. God is still our everlasting "Hope of Glory and a Strong Deliverer." Pray, talk with God that we may worship Him along with the ***"Angels Everywhere!"***

Queen Esther

Esther's name means "Star" -- well deserved, because that's what she becomes during her ten chapters in the Bible. As an orphaned Jewish girl, she wins a national beauty contest and becomes Queen of Persia, and takes a bold stand to save her people from the King's death-decree. Esther's family came from Israel, in exile under the Babylonian rule. She was raised by an elder family member, Mordecai, after the death of her parents. Esther, played a part in paving the way for the coming of the Christ. With the **"Angels Everywhere",** we know that it was the result of God's doing which allowed Esther to be chosen from among the most beautiful virgins in the land to be the Queen of Persia.

Queen Esther's Jewish identity is kept a secret, which is God's plan all along; it is now the only hope for we are to Hope only in God. In order to save the people from death, she was encouraged by her Cousin Mordecai that there was a paper written, by Haman, for her people to be destroyed. Haman, a wicked man, is appointed to the highest position as Prime Minister among the nobles; Haman, so full of evil asked the king's approval to rid the empire of God's chosen people.

Esther was so afraid because one could not go to the King unless the King says to come. Her Cousin Mordecia reminded her that this is the reason God had allowed her to become the queen in the kingdom, for such a time as this. Mordecai convinces Esther to appeal to the King, even though it is immediate death to appear before the king without an invitation. She cried and prayed along with her maids and Queen Esther was strengthened by the **"Angels Everywhere!"** Queen Esther said, ***"If I perish, I perish, I am going to see the King"*** *(Esther 4:16)*. Esther appears before the king and he permits an audience. She then invites the king and his guest to a banquet in her palace. The King with Haman as his guest appeared at the banquet feast.

Esther reveals her reason for asking the king to appear. She reveals her nationality, her danger and the presence of an enemy in the palace. A wise person knows what to say and how and when to say it (Proverbs 15:28).

She waits for the kings' response and it is truly revealed that Haman was the enemy all the time. Haman is sent to the gallows that he built to kill Mordecai. Queen Esther was obedient and saved her people from evil Haman's wicked plot planned for her people to die without a reason.

It is God's commandment that, we would do unto others as we would have done unto us. In the end, because of obedience to God's will, Queen Esther saves her people and Mordecai becomes Prime Minister of Persia. Queen Esther was helped by the **"Angels Everywhere,"** for such a time as this, to save God's people. All the people of Persia and those living in the Kingdom were happy and rejoiced. Even the King was very happy. (Read the book of Esther). Queen Esther was obedient and chosen to do God's will for His Kingdom people. Choose to do God's will.

Naomi and Ruth

God's *"providential care"* is revealed with the presence of *Angels*. The Widows: Naomi and Ruth, (a mother and her daughter-in-law) are strengthened with courage during the time of famine in the land. The Providential Care of Jehovah appears along with **"Angels Everywhere"** (Read the Book of Ruth).

The young woman Ruth did not know Jehovah personally, but followed the instructions of a woman that loved the Lord, Jehovah and through obedience, Ruth experienced Jehovah as a provider and supplier for every need. Ruth was blessed to marry, Boaz, the kinsman in the family line of Judah as preparation for the birth of a coming King -- The Messiah.

KING DAVID

It is believed there were present, Holy *Angels*, helping the young shepherd David.

David enjoyed singing and playing the harp. The youngest of seven brothers, his assignment was to care for the sheep of his father Jesse. The sheep relied on the Shepherd David to protect them from danger. David was very strong. He killed a lion and a bear, keeping the sheep safe. David was not afraid! During a battle, supernaturally, God gave David the ability to kill the tall giant Goliath with a smooth stone, found in a brook. The Shepherd boy David helped to fight in God's army against the enemy. The battle was won and Israel received the victory.

David was crowned a *"Warrior King!"* David killed the giant that came against God's Word and the Battle was won! A young shepherd boy, an obedient servant was David, a *Chosen Shepherd,* from among his brothers; David was *anointed* by the Prophet Samuel, to be the crowned King over Israel! (Read 2 Samuel 5:1-21).

God opens opportunities, allowing anyone who is obedient to Him, to lead His people and fulfill His mission. Look at the President, a joyful change forward and ordained by God! There is a call for more — *"whosoever warriors"* that will accept His mission! Warriors have ***"Angels Everywhere"*** as back up. Read for more evidence...

The Twenty-Third Psalm

The LORD is my Shepherd; I shall not want. He makes me to lie down in green pastures: He leads me beside the still waters. He restores my soul: He leads me in the paths of righteousness for His name's sake. Yea, though I walk through the valley of the shadow of death, I will fear no evil: for thou art with me; thy rod and thy staff they comfort me. Thou prepares a table before me in the presence of mine enemies: Thou anoint my head with oil; My cup runs over. Surely goodness and mercy shall follow me all the days of my life: and I will dwell in the house of the LORD Forever.

Daniel

Daniel was a teenager from Judah, in captivity under the rule of Babylon. His name means: God is my Judge! He was a visionary and prophet for over sixty years. Although sentenced to death many times, for having unshakable faith in Yahweh (God), his life was saved because he was endowed with God's *Angelic* wisdom for the interpretation of dreams and ability to read that strange *hand writing* on the wall!

It is believed that here were also mighty ***"Angels Everywhere!"*** Daniel, a young man, believed Jehovah, and would not worship any idols. An idol is anything

that we worship and enjoy much more than the worship of Jehovah. Not agreeing to worship an idol, Daniel was thrown into a Lion's Den. In that Lion's Den there was an encounter with the *Lion of all lions,* the **"Lion of Judah,"** with *Angelic* protection (Read Daniel). It is written: Believe in the Lord Jehovah, (Jehovah is another name for God).

Do not bow your head to give honor to any object or thing that takes the place of our Creator, the Lord God Jehovah. Even when it is fun and play time, God has full view of our activities. True worship is in His Spirit of love at all times. Do what is written in the Bible and the *lion of evil* will not desire to eat you, because you are protected by God and His *"Angels Everywhere." Angels* are ministering spirits (Hebrews 1:13-14). It is written in the Bible and is so.

There are other Angel witnesses: With anger, King Nebuchadnezzar commanded the Brothers Shadrach, Meshach and Abednego to be cast in a fiery furnace because they would not serve idols or worship the golden image when hearing the signal of idol music. Because they had a direct connection with the Creator in prayer, even in that fiery furnace, with walls of fire, in their presence were *"Angels Everywhere"— The Angel of protection,* stood with them. (Daniel 3:13-28). In a fiery furnace, they were not burned, not even the smell of smoke was upon them. [Note: Read Revelation 19:17 – 21:7-8 regarding *the lake of fire reservation*].

The **Messenger Angels** visited many chosen to do God's will. Just to name a few: the **Archangel Gabriel** - the Exalted Messenger of God, whose name means **"The Strength of God".** At the Last Judgment, the end of time as we know it, the **Archangel Gabriel** will blow a sacred trumpet horn and each of us shall be changed. (1 Corinthians 15:51-52). We will be transformed and become as God is: —Light". The **Archangel Gabriel** also served as a communicator and mediator, announcing the births of both John the Baptist and Jesus Christ. (Read Luke 1:26-40)

The **Archangel Michael,** studies reveals that his presence is the closest to the Lord and his name means, *"Like unto God."* Both serve as powerful spirit-beings along with *"Angels Everywhere"* protecting and guarding against forces of darkness (those who seek to do harm to God's people). Therefore we must always pray to God.

It is written that the **Angel Gabriel** visits Mary, (Read: Luke 1:26 – 40), engaged to be married to Joseph (Luke 1:27) and said to her: —Hail Mary, thou art highly favored among women. You shall have a child by the Holy Spirit!. (Read Luke 1:31) write the name of the child: _____.

The **Angel Gabriel** had already visited her cousin, Elizabeth, (and her husband, Zacharias) who prayed to have a child (Read Luke 1:5-7 also Luke1:8-12). Look it up in the Bible. Their child's name is _____(Read Luke 1:13).

The **Angel Gabriel** assisted Mary in Galilee, because she was so afraid, now with child, and had never been with a man. The *"Angels Everywhere,"* came and helped Mary by allowing Joseph to have a dream. In God there is no fear.

Joseph had a dream and he was also visited by the Angel Gabriel. After the visit by the Angel Gabriel, Joseph accepts the will of the Lord and God the Son is given (Isaiah 9:6).

Shepherds abiding in the fields saw a — Heavenly Host of *"Angels Everywhere!"* (Luke 2:8-20) and came to worship the new born King.

"The *Angels Everywhere* assisted God the Son..."

"For God So loved the World that he gave his only begotten son, that Whosoever believes in Him should not perish but have everlasting life (John 3:16). God came to earth as His Son, Jesus, who is the Christ. Jesus is the Anointed Son of God. The Creator's will for all to be redeemed was rejected by men.

In the Garden of Gethsemane, the Son of God, Jesus, prayed *"not my will but thy will be done"* (Luke 22:43). When arrested, (Matthew 26:53) Jesus had the power to call "twelve legions of *Angels*" (estimate of 72,000 *Angels*). But rather than fighting Jesus surrendered His will, that we are now free to worship God. The *"Angels Everywhere"* strengthen God the Son, Jesus to endure the pain and suffering on the cross that we might have life more abundantly.

The Bible says that all the people yelled loudly saying: Crucify Him! His Mother Mary was so sad, for she could not help him, Jesus was innocent, but understood His purpose and submitted to the will of God, the Father. Jesus was falsely accused without a trial, receiving a sentence of death by crucifixion, and hung on a cross. His death on the cross had to happen to save God's people from sin. Also fulfilling the promise for mankind to have a right relationship with fellowship in God.

Sin (S. I. N. – Self In Need) is that which is wrong, and hurts us for our sinful actions do not please the Creator, God. He gave His life willingly that those who believe in Him will live and be free to worship and do God's will. Whatever is done, if it is not right, a believer may pray to God and according to His will, He will make whatever is wrong right. Without God, when doing that which is not right other things happen, called consequences with punishment.

Only through the Son with the power of the Holy Spirit are believers able to do what is required and are able to live free eternally from the bondage of death. Jesus died on the cross and was buried in a borrowed grave. The dark grave could not hold Him because He is the Light of the world. He arose victorious with resurrection power (John 8:12).

Believers are to pray every day and give thanks to God. All of God's promises are true and faithful. Give Thanks to God for He created and sends His holy *Angels* to guide and protect us. In His presence there are **"Angels Everywhere!"** Remember, to pray at all times. God keeps us strong to do His will with the power of His Holy Spirit.

God says believers are to be prayerful, having an attitude filled with gratitude for we now live in Him. It is written in God's Holy book, that there times we do wrong, it is immediately that we pray, talk with God, ask His forgiveness of everything done wrong, and He forgives. He hears all that we say and also answers our prayers and gives us the strength to be strong in Him.

Believers are Mighty warriors of faith. *Through Christ we can do all things!* As followers of Jesus Christ, we too, like the *Angels* are always in the presence of God. It is with a heart of thanksgiving that we always give praises to God for what He did on the Cross, making believers His Righteousness. Now believers are His children of Light. Allow your Light to shine big, by doing good, that others might also believe in Him. God loves each of us that do what He says as written in His Holy book. Love everyone, for God is love, and we are also able to be full of His love. Believers have the light of Jesus within and represent Him now as the righteous. God gave the life of His Son, Jesus, so others might live and be free. Because of what God did in His Son, we are free to be all that God has created us to be.

One day soon the voice of the *"Archangel"* will sound the — Trump of God, (1 Thessalonians 4:15-17). We do not know exactly when, where, or the hour, but He shall return. All believers *wait on the Lord,* for his appearing, along with the ***"Angels Everywhere!"*** ***Everyone that believes will be caught up (also called "rapture")*** with the Lord in the middle of the air. Keep looking up, for every eye shall see Him. Acceptance by Faith, believe in the Lord, with His ***"Angels Everywhere",*** always near to help. As a "Child of the King," believers are never alone. It is now by faith, believing what God says — be ready. He shall come quickly, and we will forever be with the Lord and saved from death. Be ready now.

The ***"Angels Everywhere"*** supports us to do God's work in sharing this news with others that we are to prepare to meet the Lord, face to face. We are created to fulfill **His purpose** while on earth. Believe in Him, and know it is true, that nothing shall separate any from the love of the Lord. ***God loves unconditionally and gives everlasting life.*** Whatever happens, give thanks and remember (Proverbs 3:5-6): NKJV — *Trust in the LORD with all your heart, and lean not on your own understanding; In all your ways acknowledge Him, And He shall direct your paths."*

Believe that God created us to worship Him and all around are His Holy *Angels.*

His angelic evidence, as written, is the absolute truth:

BELIEVE – there are

"Angels Everywhere!"

(Sing a Praise and Worship Song...)

All Day and All Night! The *"Angels* Everywhere"

are Looking and Watching Over Me, Over Me, Over Me!

It is all Day, and All Night -- Yes, the *"Angels Everywhere!"*,

Keep a looking and watching over me, and watching over you!

Hallelujah! (Repeat – All...) There are *"Angels* Everywhere!"

Watching over me and watching over you...!

24